HIGH VOICE, LOW VOICE, AND PIANO

TRADITIONAL SACRED DUETS
18 Songs

COMPILED BY JOAN FREY BOYTIM

ISBN 978-1-4234-9240-5

HAL•LEONARD®
CORPORATION
7777 W. BLUEMOUND RD. P.O. BOX 13819 MILWAUKEE, WI 53213

In Australia Contact:
Hal Leonard Australia Pty. Ltd.
4 Lentara Court
Cheltenham, Victoria, 3192 Australia
Email: ausadmin@halleonard.com.au

Visit Hal Leonard Online at
www.halleonard.com

PREFACE

Many church choirs have singers who have studied voice in the past or are presently taking lessons. Many would love to sing in their church with a partner but not as a soloist. This volume of 18 duets is intended to provide a compilation of familiar as well as relatively unknown and previously out of print sacred material for church, retirement homes, community use, as well as studio recitals.

For many years I have used choral two-part sacred octavos in addition to selections from the few duet collections available. This collection provides a new sacred duet source for singers and teachers. The duets range from easy to moderate levels of difficulty.

This compilation contains some frequently requested duets, such as, "I Waited for the Lord," "O Divine Redeemer," "The King of Love My Shepherd Is," and "The Lord Is My Shepherd." Several Baroque and Classical favorites included are: "As the Hart Panteth" and "Give Ear Unto Me," both by Marcello; "O Lovely Peace" by Handel; "Ave, Verum" by Mozart; and "Hear Us, O Savior" by Rameau.

For beginning duet pairs, some very easy selections are: "Come, Let Us All Rejoicing," "God Is a Spirit," "Like As the Hart," and "Songs of Praise the Angels Sang." Two out of print duets which are particularly pleasant additions to the repertoire are: "Savior, Like a Shepherd Lead Us" by Jones and "Lord, Speak to Me" by Roberts.

May using selections from this volume in church, public performances, and recitals bring joy to both the singers and those who attend the performances.

Joan Frey Boytim
June, 2010

CONTENTS

AS THE HART PANTETH

Psalm 42:1, 15

Benedetto Marcello
Arranged by W. H. Longhurst

Andante

High Voice:

As the hart ___ pant - eth, as the hart ___ pant - eth af - ter ___ the ___

wa - ter-brooks, so my soul long - eth af - ter thee, ___ O God, af -

Low Voice:

As the hart ___ pant - eth, as the hart ___ pant - eth af -

*Optional ending

COME, BLESSED SAVIOR
(Ave, Maria)

Traditional

Camille Saint-Saëns

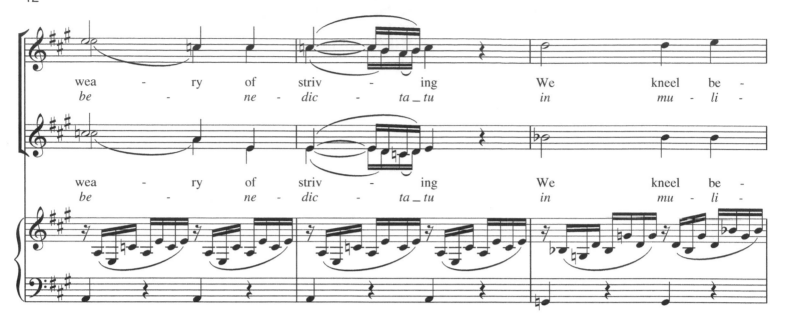

wea - ry of striv - ing We kneel be -
be - ne - dic - ta _ tu in mu - li -

fore _____ thee, O bless - ed Sav - ior,
e - ri - bus et be - ne - dic - tus

Grant us now thy peace and mer -
fruc - tus ven - tris tu - i Je -

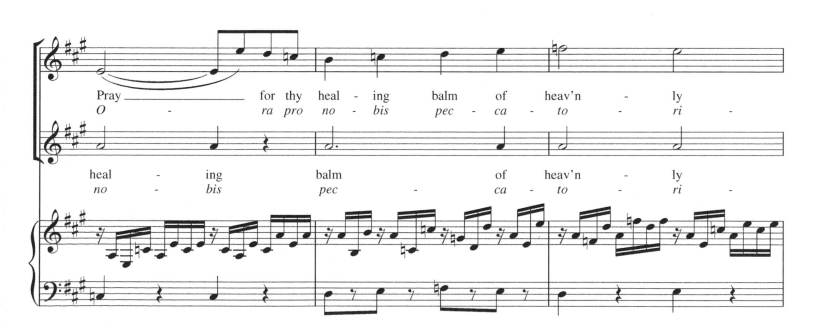

14

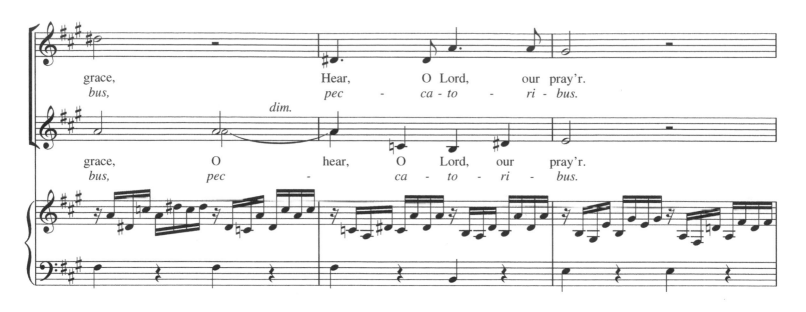

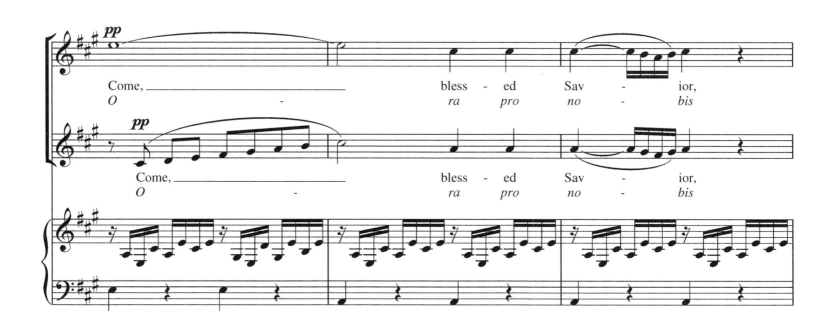

COME, LET US ALL REJOICING

Robert M. Offord

James C. Warhurst

not for nought we cry, For ev-'ry want we bring him, He gives a rich sup-

seek him, nor cry, For ev-'ry want we bring him, He gives a rich sup-

Fine   **Poco lento**

ply, For ev-ery want we bring him, He gives a rich sup-ply.

ply, For ev-ery want we bring him, He gives a rich sup-ply.

Low Voice: (or High Voice)

Still, on his word be-

liev- ing, Will_ we new_ fa-vors_ seek; And fa- vors new re- ceiv- ing, Our_

con- stant_ prais- es speak, For mer - cies nev-er end- ing, Let glad thanks-giv-ings

High Voice:

rise, And prayers and prais-es blend-ing, To - geth- er reach the skies, And prayers and prais-es

Tempo I

D.C.

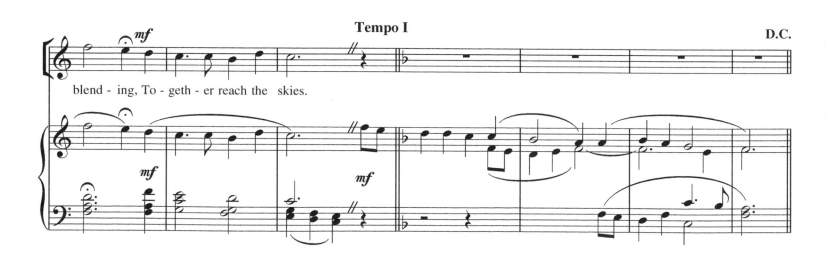

blend - ing, To - geth - er reach the skies.

GIVE EAR UNTO ME

Psalm 17

Benedetto Marcello
Figured bass arranged by Vincent Novello

GOD IS A SPIRIT

John 4:23b-24

William Sterndale Bennett

HEAR US, O SAVIOR
(Ave, Maria)

Traditional

Jean-Philippe Rameau

LIKE AS THE HART

Psalm 42:1, 6, 15

Vincent Novello
Arranged by H. Elliot Button

IS IT NOTHING TO YOU?

Lamentations 1:12; Isaiah 53:5;
John 3:16

Myles B. Foster

Is it noth-ing to you, all ye that pass __ by, is it noth-

He was wound-ed for our trans-gres-sions, He was bruis-ed for

ing? He was wound-ed for our trans-gres-sions, He was bruis-ed for

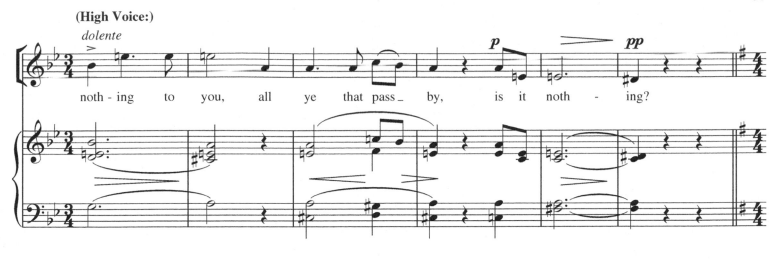

I WAITED FOR THE LORD

from *Symphony No. 2 in B-flat Major, "Lobgesang," Op. 52*

Felix Mendelssohn

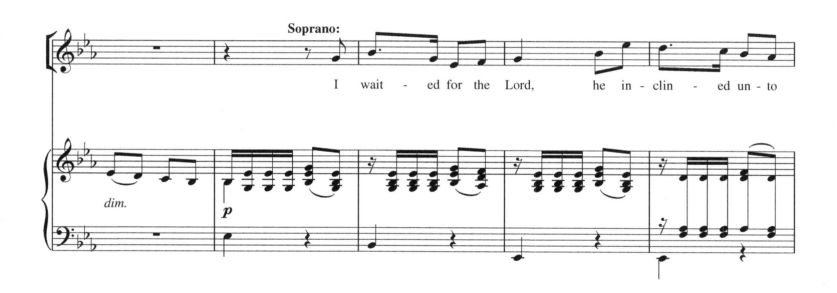

plaint; I wait-ed for the Lord, he in-clin-ed un-to

me, and heard my com-plaint, and _ heard my com-

plaint. O bless'd are they that hope and trust in the

Lord.

me, to me. O bless'd _____ are they that

clin - ed un - to me. O bless'd _____ are they that

ppp

hope and trust, that hope _____ and trust in him.

hope and trust, that hope _____ and trust in him.

pp

p

Ped.

※

JESUS, SAVIOR
(Ave, Verum)

Traditional

Wolfgang Amadeus Mozart

Andante

High Voice:

Je - sus, Sav - ior word in - car - nate, Thou art
A - ve, ve - rum cor - pus na - tum, na - tum

Low Voice:

Je - sus, Sav - ior word in - car - nate, Thou art
A - ve, ve - rum cor - pus na - tum, na - tum

tru - ly born the Son of God, Thy dear bod - y, suf - fered cruel - ly The
De Ma - ri - a vir - gi - ne, ve - re pas - sum, im - mo - la - tum In

tru - ly born the Son of God, Thy dear bod - y, suf - fered cruel - ly The
De Ma - ri - a vir - gi - ne, ve - re pas - sum, im - mo - la - tum In

cross thou didst bear for us;
cru - ce pro ho - mi - ne;

cross thou didst bear for us;
cru - ce pro ho - mi - ne;

O Je-sus hear_ us! O__ Je-sus spare_ us! O Je-sus pit - y thy chil - dren!
O Je-su dul - cis! O__ Je-su pi - e! O Je-su fi - li Ma - ri - ae!

O Je-sus hear_ us! O__ Je-sus spare_ us! O Je-sus pit - y thy chil - dren!
O Je-su dul - cis! O__ Je-su pi - e! O Je-su fi - li Ma - ri - ae!

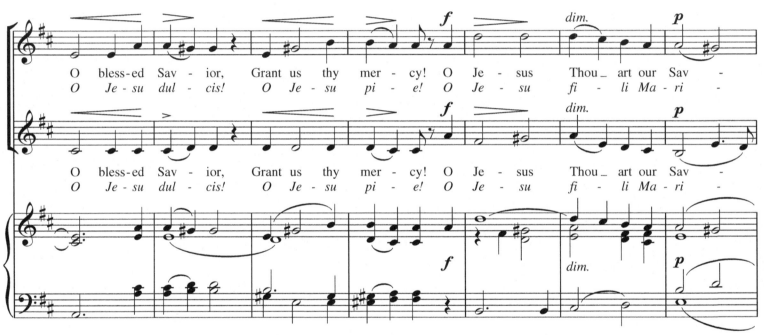

O bless-ed Sav - ior, Grant us thy mer - cy! O Je - sus Thou_ art our Sav -
O Je-su dul - cis! O Je-su pi - e! O Je - su fi - li Ma-ri

O bless-ed Sav - ior, Grant us thy mer - cy! O Je - sus Thou_ art our Sav -
O Je-su dul - cis! O Je-su pi - e! O Je - su fi - li Ma-ri

ior,   Teach us to love _ thee, Teach _ us to know _ thee,
ae!   O Je-su dul - cis! O__ Je-su pi - e!

ior,   Teach us to love   thee, Teach us to know _ thee,
ae!   O Je-su dul - cis! O Je-su pi - e!

We thy weak chil - dren im - plore thee, Save us, we pray thee
O Je - su fi - li Ma - ri - ae! Tu no - bis mi - se -

We thy weak chil - dren im - plore thee, Save us, we pray thee
O Je - su fi - li Ma - ri - ae! Tu no - bis mi - se -

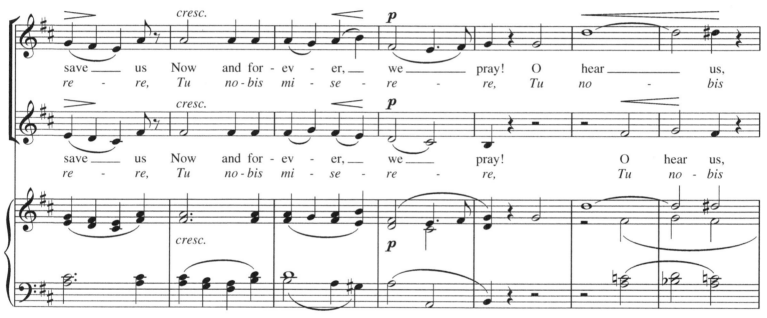

save us Now and for - ev - er, we pray! O hear us,
re - re, Tu no - bis mi - se - re - re, Tu no - bis

save us Now and for - ev - er, we pray! O hear us,
re - re, Tu no - bis mi - se - re - re, Tu no - bis

hear and help us: A - men! A - men!
mi - se - re - re: A - men! A - men!

hear and help us: A - men! A - men!
mi - se - re - re: A - men! A - men!

THE KING OF LOVE MY SHEPHERD IS

Henry W. Baker

Harry Rowe Shelley

verse and fool - ish oft I stray'd, But yet in love he sought me, And

on his shoul - der gen - tly laid, And home re - joic - ing brought ___ me.

Low Voice: *p*

In death's dark vale I fear no

THE LORD IS MY SHEPHERD

W.S. Passmore
Psalm 23, paraphrased

Henry Smart

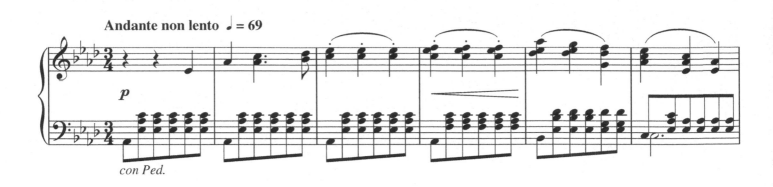

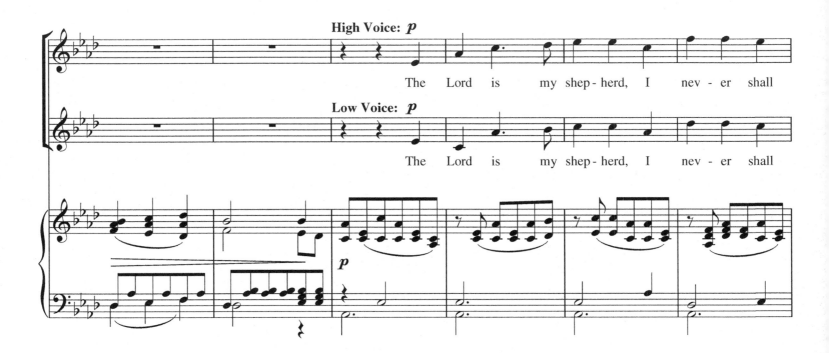

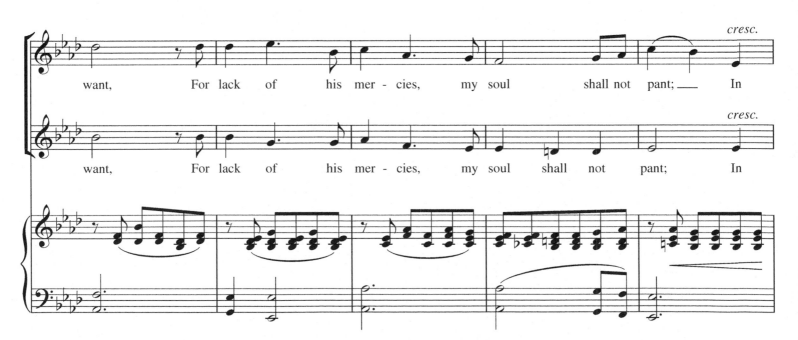

Yea, though I pass through death's dark val - ley and shade, I
bids me to take; Yea, though I pass through death's dark shade,

will not by e - vil be ev - er dis - may'd, I will not by e - vil be
I will not by e - vil be ev - er dis - may'd, by e - vil be

ev - er dis - may'd. The Lord is my shep - herd, I nev - er shall
ev - er dis - may'd. The Lord is my shep - herd, I nev - er shall

colla voci

pres - ence of __ foes, My head thou a - noint - est, my cup ov - er - flows: __ Thy

pres - ence of __ foes, My head thou a - noint - est, my cup ov - er - flows; __

good - ness and __ mer - cy shall fol - low me still, __ While life's ear - nest

du - ties I dai - ly ful - fil; Till joy - ous my __ spir - it shall

My __ spir - it shall __

LORD, SPEAK TO ME

Frances R. Havergall

J.E. Roberts

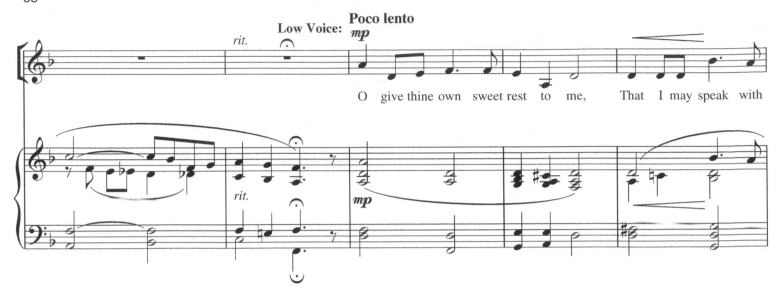

O give thine own sweet rest to me, That I may speak with

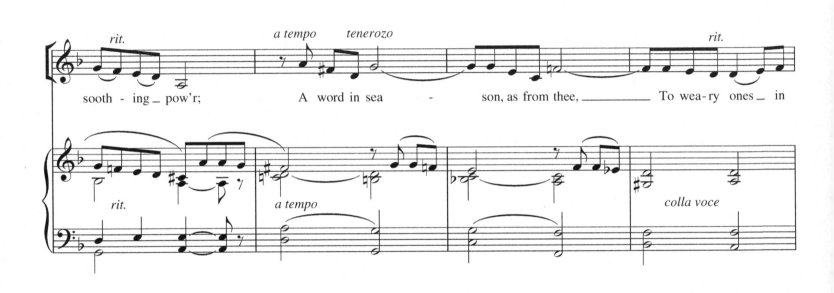

sooth - ing — pow'r; A word in sea - son, as from thee, _____ To wea - ry ones — in

need - ful hour. O fill me with thy full - ness, _ Lord, Un-

til my ver - y __ heart o'er-flow In kin-dling thought and glow - ing word, __ Thy

til my ver - y __ heart o'er-flow In __ kin-dling thought and glow - ing word, __ Thy

love to tell, __ thy __ praise to show, In __ kin-dling thought and glow - ing word, __

love to tell, thy __ praise to show, In kin-dling thought and glow - ing word, __

Thy love to tell, thy praise _____ to show.

Thy love to tell, thy __ praise _____ to show.

O, DIVINE REDEEMER
(Parce, domine)
Prayer

Charles Gounod

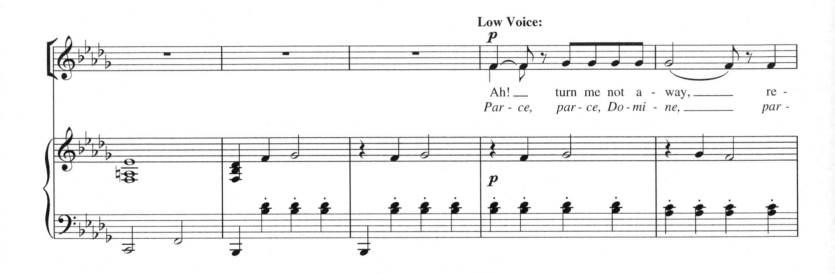

O HOW AMIABLE
ARE THY DWELLINGS

Psalm 84:1, 2, 4, 5, 13

J.H. Maunder

High Voice: *f*

O_ how a - mia-ble are_ thy_ dwell-ings, thou Lord_ of

Low Voice: *f*

O_ how a - mia - ble are_ thy_ dwell-ings, thou Lord_ of

hosts,_ Thou Lord_ of hosts! My soul hath a de - sire and long - ing to

hosts,_ Thou Lord of hosts! My soul hath a de - sire, and

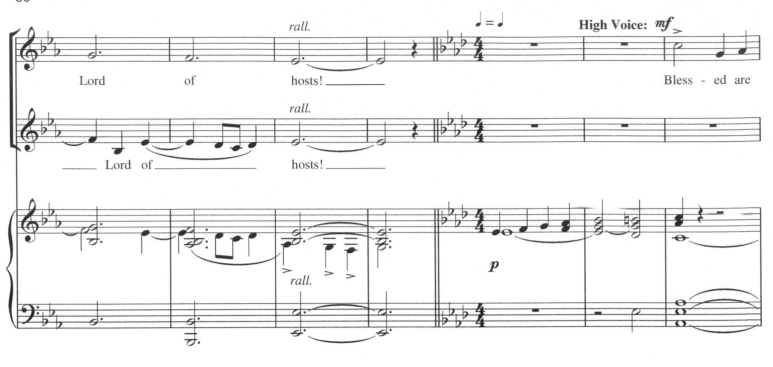

Lord of hosts! _____ Bless - ed are

_____ Lord of _____ hosts! _____

they that dwell in thy house, they will be al - way prais - ing thee, be

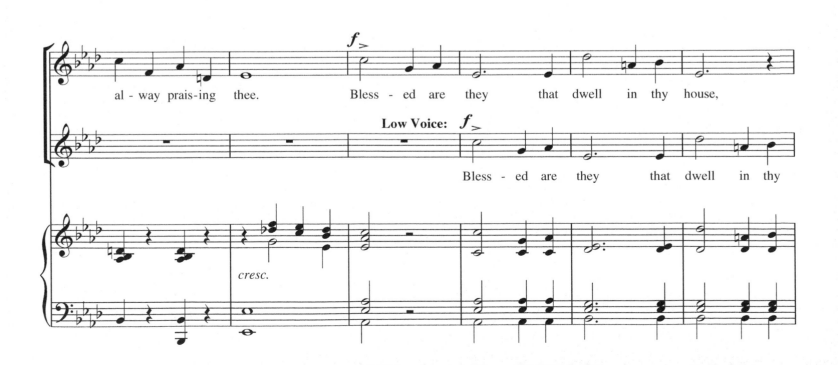

al - way prais-ing thee. Bless - ed are they that dwell in thy house,

Bless - ed are they that dwell in thy

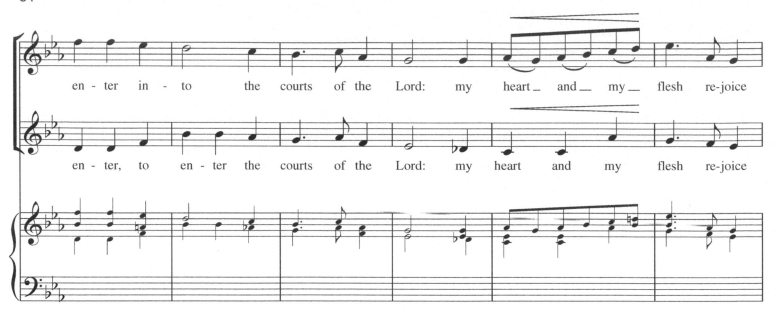

enter in-to the courts of the Lord: my heart _ and _ my _ flesh re-joice

enter, to en-ter the courts of the Lord: my heart and my flesh re-joice

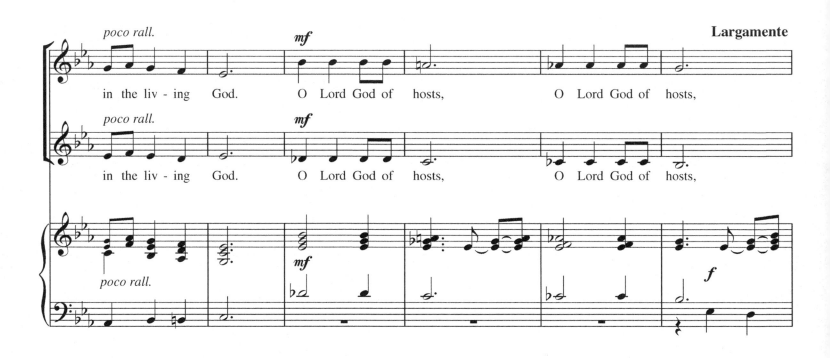

in the liv-ing God. O Lord God of hosts, O Lord God of hosts,

in the liv-ing God. O Lord God of hosts, O Lord God of hosts,

bless-ed is _ the man that put-teth his trust, his trust _ in thee.

bless-ed is the man that put-teth his trust, his trust _ in thee.

O LOVELY PEACE

from *Judas Maccabaeus*

George Frideric Handel

Allegro

mp

High Voice:

O love - ly Peace, _ with plen - ty crown'd, _

p

O love - ly, love - ly Peace, _ Come, spread _ thy _ bless - ings, thy _ bless - ings

SONGS OF PRAISE THE ANGELS SANG

James Montgomery

Thomas Attwood

bove, Learn - ing here, by faith ___ and love, Songs of
ploy, Then, a - midst e - ter - nal joy, Songs of

bove, Learn - ing here, ___ by faith ___ and love, ___ Songs ___ of ___
ploy, Then ___ a - midst ___ e - ter - nal joy, ___ Songs ___ of ___

praise ___ to ___ sing ___ a - bove.
praise ___ their ___ pow'rs em - ploy.

praise ___ to ___ sing ___ a - bove.
praise ___ their ___ pow'rs em - ploy.

SAVIOUR, LIKE A SHEPHERD LEAD US

Anonymous

Walter Howe Jones

Ear - ly let us seek thy fa - vor, Ear - ly let us do thy will; Bless - ed Lord and

Ear - ly let us seek thy fa - vor, Ear - ly let us do thy will; Bless - ed Lord and

on - ly sav - iour, With thy love our bos - oms fill: Bless - ed Je - sus, Bless - ed Je - sus,

on - ly sav - iour, With thy love our bos - oms fill: Bless - ed Je - sus, Bless - ed Je - sus,

thou hast loved us, love us still, thou hast loved us, love us still.

thou hast loved us, love us still, thou hast loved us, love us still.